When The Clock Strikes On Christmas Eve

Written by : Lisa Ferland

Illustrated by : Pei Jen

When the clock strikes one,
you're having such great fun!

Skates on ice, oh, how they glide.
Wintertime is best outside.

When the clock strikes three,
it's time to deck your tree.

Decorate with shiny things,
tiny stars, and angel wings.

When the clock strikes four,
there's knocking at your door.

Cousins play hide-and-seek,
aunts and uncles kiss your cheek.

Be sure to count the candy canes on each page
for more counting fun!

Can you find the mice family living in the house?

Please leave a review!

We love our readers!
Tag us on social media with pictures of your books
#whentheclockstrikes

 Instagram:
@lisaferland_
@toffeefingerart

Become a VIP Reader and subscribe at:
www.lisaferland.com/when-the-clock-strikes-series

If you loved this book you'll also love
When the Clock Strikes on Halloween

Dedicated to everyone who counts the hours until Christmas. — LF
Dedicated to my parents and my Toffee. — PJ

Copyright © 2019 Lisa Ferland

All rights reserved.

No part of this publication may be reproduced, distributed, or transmitted in any form or by any means, including photocopying, recording, or other electronic or mechanical methods, without the prior written permission of the publisher, except in the case of brief quotations embodied in critical reviews and certain other noncommercial uses permitted by copyright law.

Smart elves will ask for permission and can contact the publisher at:
www.lisaferland.com

Paperback ISBN: 978-0-9970624-6-5
Hardcover ISBN: 978-91-985805-0-1

About the Author

Lisa Ferland is a writer and mother to a ninja warrior and a dancing firefly. She and her family live in Sweden but she's called many places home. Connect with Lisa at lisaferland.com.

About the Illustrator

Pei Jen is a Malaysian illustrator who loves bringing magic into children's books. She has loved drawing since she was a kid and experiments learning new artistic styles in both fantasy and realism.
You can follow her work on Instagram at @toffeefingerart.

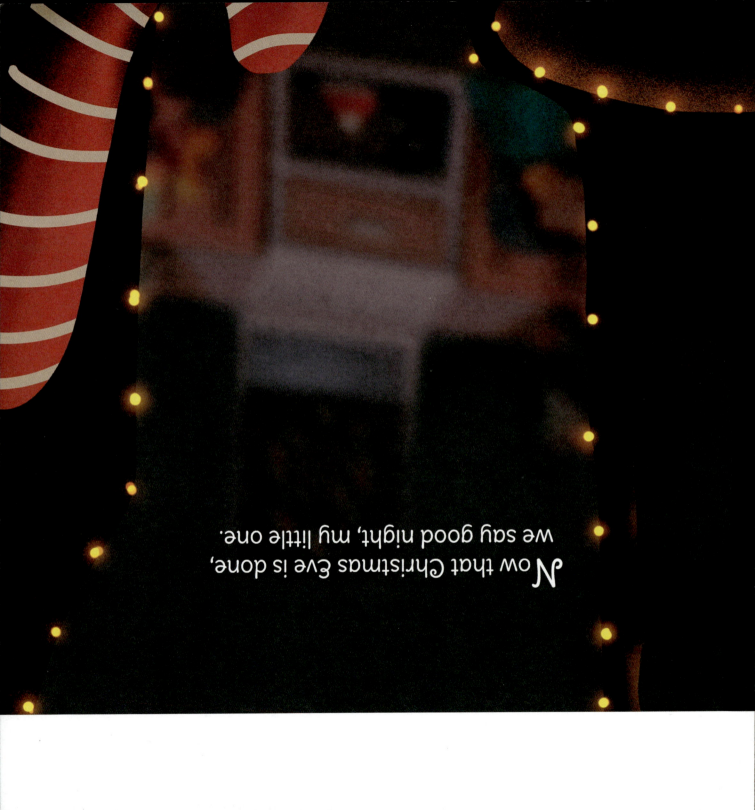

Now that Christmas Eve is done, we say good night, my little one.

When the clock strikes nine,
your eyes begin to shine.

Thinking of the fun to come,
toys and books for everyone.

When the clock strikes ten,
you set out Santa's cookie men.

Gingerbread and chocolate chip,
add some milk for him to sip.

When the clock strikes eleven,
your bed's a sleeping heaven.

Dream a dream as sweet as you
'cause on Christmas, dreams come true.

When the clock strikes twelve, your house is calm—it's midnight.

When you're sleeping, tucked in tight Santa brings you gifts tonight.

When the clock strikes five,
the Christmas spirit comes alive.

By the fire, warm your nose,
wrapped in blankets head to toes.

When the clock strikes six,
you light your candlesticks.

Flames are dancing, oh so bright,
the candles twinkle through the night.

When the clock strikes seven,
you meet an elf named Kevin.

Funny, cute, and super smart,
Kevin toots a sneaky fart.

When the clock strikes eight,
you fill your dinner plate.

Buttered rolls and turkey roast,
it's Grandma's pie you love the most.

Made in the USA
Coppell, TX
05 December 2020